THE ADVENTURES OF
ISABEL

Ogden Nash

Pictures by

James Marshall

Little, Brown and Company Boston New York Toronto London

First Paperback Edition

Library of Congress Cataloging-in-Publication Data

Nash, Ogden, 1902–1971.
    The adventures of Isabel / Ogden Nash ; pictures by James Marshall.
    —1st ed.
    p.   cm.
    Summary: The feisty Isabel defeats giants, witches, and other
    threatening creatures with ease.
    ISBN 0-316-59874-7 (hc)
    ISBN 0-316-59883-6 (pb)
    1. Children's poetry, American. [1. Heroines—Poetry.   2. American
    poetry.] I. Marshall, James, 1942– ill. II. Title.
    PS3527.A637A68   1991   90-13284
    811'.52—dc20

10 9 8 7 6 5 4 3 2 1

WOR

Published simultaneously in Canada
by Little, Brown & Company (Canada) Limited

Printed in the United States of America

THE ADVENTURES OF

ISABEL

Isabel met an enormous bear,

Isabel, Isabel, didn't care;
The bear was hungry, the bear was ravenous,
The bear's big mouth was cruel and cavernous.

The bear said, "Isabel, glad to meet you,

How do, Isabel, now I'll eat you!"

Isabel, Isabel, didn't worry,

Isabel didn't scream or scurry.

She washed her hands and she straightened her hair up,

Then Isabel quietly ate the bear up.

Once in a night as black as pitch
Isabel met a wicked old witch.

The witch's face was cross and wrinkled,
The witch's gums with teeth were sprinkled.
"Ho ho, Isabel!" the old witch crowed,
"I'll turn you into an ugly toad!"

Isabel, Isabel, didn't worry,

Isabel didn't scream or scurry.

She showed no rage and showed no rancor,

But she turned the witch into milk and drank her.

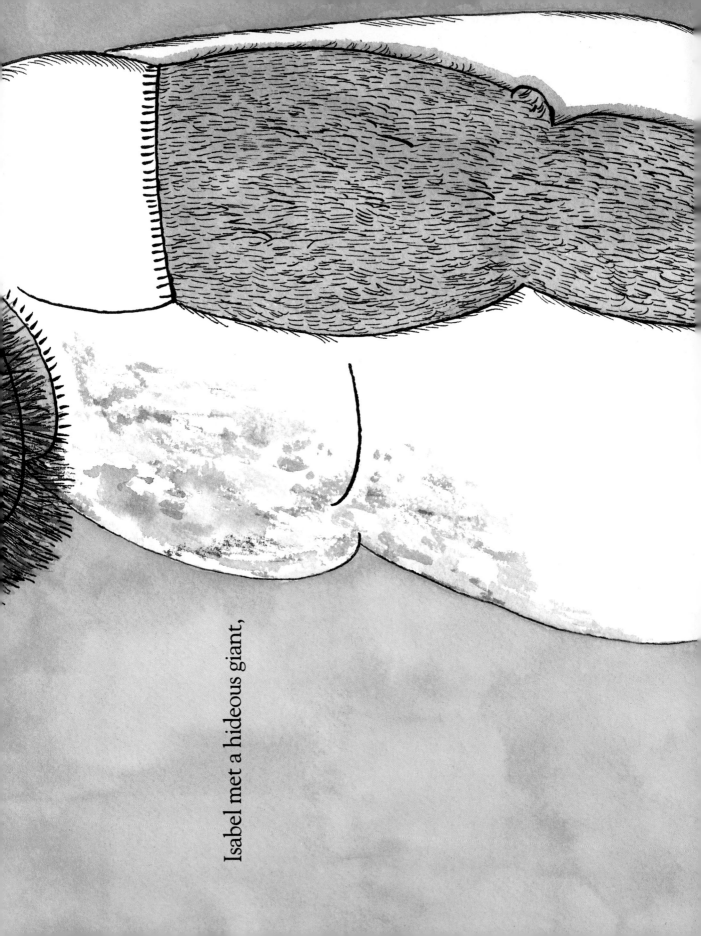

Isabel met a hideous giant,

Isabel continued self-reliant.

The giant was hairy, the giant was horrid,

He had one eye in the middle of his forehead.

"Good morning, Isabel," the giant said,

"I'll grind your bones to make my bread."

Isabel, Isabel, didn't worry,
Isabel didn't scream or scurry.
She nibbled the zwieback that she always fed off,
And when it was gone, she cut the giant's head off.

Isabel met a troublesome doctor,

He punched and he poked till he really shocked her.

The doctor's talk was of coughs and chills

And the doctor's satchel bulged with pills.

The doctor said unto Isabel,

"Swallow this, it will make you well."

Isabel, Isabel, didn't worry,
Isabel didn't scream or scurry.
She took those pills from the pill concocter,
And Isabel calmly cured the doctor.

Isabel once was asleep in bed
When a horrible dream crawled into her head.
It was worse than a dinosaur, worse than a shark,
Worse than an octopus oozing in the dark.
"Boo!" said the dream, with a dreadful grin,
"I'm going to scare you out of your skin!"

Isabel, Isabel, didn't worry,
Isabel didn't scream or scurry.
Isabel had a cleverer scheme;
She just woke up and fooled that dream.

Whenever *you* meet a bugaboo
Remember what Isabel used to do.

Don't scream when the bugaboo says "Boo!"
Just look it in the eye and say, "Boo to you!"
That's how to banish a bugaboo;
Isabel did it and you can too!